ROBOTICS ENGINEERING
AND Our Automated World

ENGINEERING IN ACTION

Crabtree Publishing Company

www.crabtreebooks.com

Rebecca Sjonger

Crabtree Publishing Company

www.crabtreebooks.com

Author: Rebecca Sjonger
Series research and development: Reagan Miller
Editorial director: Kathy Middleton
Photo research: James Nixon
Editors: Paul Humphrey, James Nixon, and
Philip Gebhardt
Proofreader: Wendy Scavuzzo
Layout: sprout.uk.com
Cover design and logo: Margaret Amy Salter
Production coordinator and prepress technician:
Margaret Amy Salter
Print coordinator: Katherine Berti

Consultant: Carolyn de Cristofano, M.Ed. STEM
consultant, Professional Development Director of
Engineering is Elementary (2005–2008)

Production coordinated by Discovery Books

Photographs:
Alamy: pp. 19 top (Randy Duchaine), 20 (EPA/ALEX
HOFFORD), 25 bottom-right (EPA/SVEN HOPPE),
29 bottom (Ryan Etter).
Bigstock: pp. 4 top (ndoeljindoel), 4 bottom (Sasin Tip-
chai), 6 (georgina198), 9 bottom (aireo), 12 top (gogian),
27 (trans961).
Getty Images: pp. 5 (Lane Turner/The Boston Globe),
10 (Larry Burrows/The LIFE Picture Collection), 11 top
(Ralph Crane/The LIFE Picture Collection).
Hilton Worldwide: p. 17 bottom (Photo courtesy of Green
Buzz Agency/Feature Photo Service for IBM).
MIT: p. 8 top (Jose-Luis Olivares).
NASA/JPL-Caltech: pp. 15 top, 15 bottom, 18, 21 top, 22, 23.
Shutterstock: p. 28 bottom (Irina Kozorog).
Wikimedia: pp. 7 top (Humanrobo), 8 bottom (NASA),
9 top (DARPA), 11 bottom (UL Digital Library), 12
bottom (Hidden Ocean 2005 Expedition: NOAA Office
of Ocean Exploration), 13 left (DVIDSHUB), 13 right
(Mike1024), 14 (NASA), 16 top (NASA), 16 bottom
(NASA/JPL-Caltech/Malin Space Science Systems),
17 top-left (Science Museum London/Science and
Society Picture Library), 17 top-right, 19 bottom
(NASA/Kim Shiflett), 21 bottom (NASA), 24 (NASA/
JPL-Caltech/MSSS), 25 top (World Wide Gifts), 25
bottom-left (The White House from Washington, DC),
28 top (Cmglee), 29 top (Michael Shick).

All other images by Shutterstock

Library and Archives Canada Cataloguing in Publication

Sjonger, Rebecca, author
Robotics engineering and our automated world / Rebecca
Sjonger.

(Engineering in action)
Includes index.
Issued in print and electronic formats.
ISBN 978-0-7787-7537-9 (hardback).--
ISBN 978-0-7787-7541-6 (paperback).--
ISBN 978-1-4271-1786-1 (html)

1. Robotics--Juvenile literature. 2. Engineering--Juvenile
literature. I. Title. II. Series: Engineering in action
(St. Catharines, Ont.)

TJ211.2.S56 2016   j629.8'92   C2016-903293-0
                                            C2016-903294-9

Library of Congress Cataloging-in-Publication Data

Names: Sjonger, Rebecca, author.
Title: Robotics engineering and our automated world / Rebecca
Sjonger.
Description: St. Catharines, Ontario ; New York, New York :
Crabtree Publishing Company, [2016] | Series: Engineering in
action | Includes index.
Identifiers: LCCN 2016027282 (print) | LCCN 2016028601 (ebook)
| ISBN 9780778775379 (reinforced library binding : alk. paper)
| ISBN 9780778775416 (pbk. : alk. paper)
| ISBN 9781427117861 (Electronic HTML)
Subjects: LCSH: Robotics--Juvenile literature. | Technological
innovations--Juvenile literature.
Classification: LCC TJ211.2 .S56 2016 (print) | LCC TJ211.2
(ebook) | DDC 629.8/92--dc23
LC record available at https://lccn.loc.gov/2016027282

Crabtree Publishing Company
www.crabtreebooks.com   1-800-387-7650

Printed in Canada/072016/EF20160630

Published in Canada
Crabtree Publishing
616 Welland Ave.
St. Catharines, ON
L2M 5V6

Published in the United States
Crabtree Publishing
PMB 59051
350 Fifth Avenue, 59th Floor
New York, New York 10118

Published in the United Kingdom
Crabtree Publishing
Maritime House
Basin Road North, Hove
BN41 1WR

Published in Australia
Crabtree Publishing
3 Charles Street
Coburg North
VIC, 3058

CONTENTS

WHAT IS ROBOTICS ENGINEERING?

People who specialize in robotics engineering are called roboticists. They design **technologies** that often do dull, dirty, or dangerous jobs. Robots excel at repetitive tasks and are commonly used in factories. Other robots are designed to take on unpleasant duties, such as maintaining sewers. Some robots work in areas that are not safe for humans, including disaster zones. Robots are also developed to go where it is difficult for people to go, such as the deepest seafloors. Roboticists think up **innovative** new ideas all the time. For example, some of them are developing tiny robots to explore and heal human bodies from the inside!

Roboticists: Some roboticists are robotics engineers, but they also come from many other fields of engineering and science. They often work as part of a team. For example, electrical engineers may develop parts that sense a robot's surroundings. Mechanical engineers often design moving robotic parts. Computer scientists **program** robots. Flip to pages 12 and 13 to read about some of the fields in which roboticists work.

Factory robots can carry out repetitive tasks with speed and accuracy.

EIGHT STEPS TO SUCCESS

Roboticists can design ways to explore remote mountains, replace **paralyzed** or missing body parts with mechanical parts, or put together a smartphone. All of these inventions are the result of the engineering design process. This series of eight steps helps roboticists design, build, and test solutions.

Steps in the design process

Define the problem

↓

Identify criteria and constraints

↓

Brainstorm ideas

↓

Select a possible solution

↓

Build a prototype

Improve the design ← → **Test the prototype**

↓

Share the solution

Dr. Breazeal (right) designed Jibo to help people in their homes. What do you think are the pros and cons of robotic companions for humans?

DR. CYNTHIA BREAZEAL

Seeing the robots in Star Wars sparked eight-year-old Cynthia Breazeal's passion for robotics. Her parents encouraged her interest in engineering. After Dr. Breazeal earned university degrees in electrical engineering and computer science, she began designing robots for use in space. In 1997, she switched to developing socially intelligent robots. They communicate with people and mimic human emotions. One of her latest inventions is Jibo. Dr. Breazeal's team created this robot to work as a helper and companion in a home setting. It can do everything from reading stories to children to helping elderly people who are confined to their homes feel connected to the outside world.

PARTS AND PROCESS

People disagree about what defines a robot—even roboticists have differing ideas. We often draw a line between robots and other machines by how much they control their own actions. In this book, robotic technologies with varying levels of control are all called robots. Many of the examples are **autonomous** robots, which function without human help. Have you ever seen a self-operating vacuum cleaner or an automatic car wash? These are autonomous robots.

A robotic vacuum cleaner.

SENSE-THINK-ACT PROCESS

Autonomous robots follow a sense-think-act process that makes them distinct from other machines. **Sensors** detect data from the robot's surroundings. Roboticists design sensors that can "feel," "hear," or "see" things such as heat, sound, or light. The incoming information goes to the robot's **control system**. It acts as the robot's brain. A computer analyzes the data and looks for instructions in its program. Commands for which actions to take then go to **actuators**. They are like muscles for robots. They move **effectors**, which are parts of the robot's body. These allow robots to affect their environment.

Sensors, a control system, and actuators work together in the sense-think-act process. Each part is equally important.

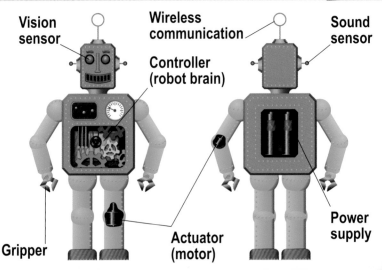

Vision sensor

Wireless communication

Sound sensor

Controller (robot brain)

Gripper

Actuator (motor)

Power supply

Artificial intelligence: Roboticists modeled the sense-think-act process based on how humans think and make decisions. People use their senses, consider the information, then take action. Unlike humans, robots need someone to program them. Robots can only do new tasks if a roboticist reprograms them. However, advances in **artificial intelligence** (**AI**) may change this. For now, robots with AI mimic, or imitate, human intelligence. Developments in AI may allow robots to learn and reprogram themselves.

Some robotics engineering is just for fun! This robot's AI allows it to play table tennis with humans.

Remote-controlled robots: Sometimes, roboticists leave one or more steps of the sense-think-act process to human operators. People can receive data from robotic sensors and analyze it. Then they decide which action to take and use remote control to tell the robot what to do. For example, a bomb-disposal robot allows a human to disable a bomb from a safe distance. Robots that follow a limited sense-think-act process are semi-autonomous. Humans control them in situations that are beyond the programming of these robots.

Bomb-disposal robots are designed to do a dangerous job, which keeps humans from harm.

SYSTEMS THINKING

Roboticists develop autonomous and remote-controlled robots in many forms. How designers choose to make a robot look depends on its intended use. Robotics engineering technologies range in size from tiny to several stories tall. Some of the most common robots are mechanical arms called manipulators. They can be jointed, **telescopic**, or snake-like. Manipulators may also be one part of a multi-part robot body. Other common robots, called **androids**, use the human body as a model. Roboticists even create robots that mimic animals. Robots may look different, but they are all systems.

Robotics engineering often borrows ideas from nature. This robot runs like a cheetah—but not quite as fast!

The Canadian Space Agency's Canadarm2 is a manipulator. The robotic arm has seven joints that help it move.

A system is a set of related parts that work together. Each system includes inputs, processes, and outputs. For example, cameras on the Canadarm manipulator took images (inputs) from the outside of **space shuttles**. Its computers stored the data for a human operator to process. This person then used the mechanical arm to perform tasks (outputs), such as building the International Space Station.

Mechatronic systems: Robots are mechatronic systems, which means they have electrical, computer, and mechanical parts that interconnect. Many systems include **subsystems** that affect one another. For example, a control system is a robotic subsystem made up of a set of computer parts. They rely on a subsystem of sensors to detect data. The control system also needs a mechanical subsystem to carry out its commands. Roboticists must be experts at designing systems for robots to function properly.

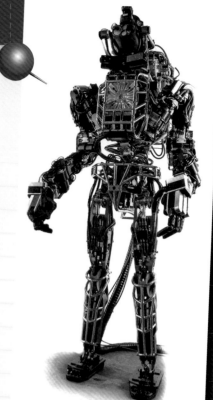

EXAMINE A SYSTEM

Play your favorite game to explore a system. Start by listing all the parts of your game, such as a board, cards, or dice. As you play, consider how each part connects to create a system. Can you identify any subsystems within your game? For example, the rules are a subsystem that includes the object of the game, instructions for playing, and how to win. Inputs and outputs are less obvious in a game system than in a mechatronic system. The resources needed to play a game, including game pieces and players' movements, are inputs. The output is a task the game performs, which may be for players to have fun or to learn teamwork.

Try changing part of your game system, such as how a player wins. Play the game again and observe the effects of changing one part of the system.

CENTURIES OF IDEAS

Do you ever dream of inventing a robot to have fun with or do chores for you? Before sensors and computers existed, this was pure fantasy. Instead, people innovated with mechanical systems. For example, they made self-moving machines called automatons that were powered by humans, wind, or water. The main function of these machines was to entertain people. Automatons often had human or animal forms.

Leonardo da Vinci designed an automaton knight in the late 1400s. A system of connected **pulleys** and gears moved its body. In the 1730s, French inventor Jacques de Vaucanson created a mechanical duck. It quacked and flapped its wings. The duck even appeared to eat by taking food into its body. Looking back, we now see automatons as the forerunners of today's robots.

Rise of the "robota"

The first use of the word "robota" was in a play in 1921. It means "forced work" in Czech. The playwright, Karel Capek, described a world in which robots did humans' jobs. Within 40 years, his vision came true. One of the first steps toward modern robots came in 1948, thanks to British robotics **pioneer** William Grey Walter. He designed some of the earliest battery-powered autonomous robots. Their official name was the Machina Speculatrix. However, the robots moved so slowly that they were called tortoises.

The outer shell of a Machina Speculatrix "tortoise" covered its control system and actuators. Outer sensors detected light and touch.

About 20 years after the Machina Speculatrix was built, a team at Stanford Research Institute created Shakey. This robot had sensors and moved with the help of a control system that took up a whole room. The computer sent information to it from a radio antenna on Shakey's head. In 1970, *Life* magazine described Shakey as "the first electronic person."

Shakey got its name because its movements were not very steady!

GEORGE DEVOL AND JOSEPH ENGELBERGER

In the early 1950s, American inventor George Devol designed the first programmable manipulator. He shared his idea with American electrical engineer and scientist Joseph Engelberger. Devol's new partner thought the jointed mechanical arm could do jobs that were dangerous for humans to do. They named their creation Unimate.

In 1961, the Unimate manipulator went to work. It welded car parts on a General Motors assembly line in New Jersey. Soon, many aspects of manufacturing were automated, or done by machines. Today, Devol and Engelberger are called the "fathers of modern robotics."

Unimate worked with extremely hot metals, which humans could not touch without being injured.

MODERN ROBOTICISTS

Robotics includes many branches of engineering, including electrical, mechanical, and systems engineering. Many modern roboticists also have backgrounds in computer science. They combine their technical skills and knowledge with creativity to come up with solutions. They must understand how each part relates to the whole design. Systems thinking requires a lot of problem solving, too. Roboticists **collaborate** and share with one another throughout the design process.

Diverse designs

Today's roboticists work in many fields. They may design **drones** that kids can fly or alarm clocks that roll away after someone hits the snooze button. On farms, roboticists are automating processes such as milking cows with robots. In hospitals, autonomous robots can move around the building and deliver supplies. On page 28, you'll find out how roboticists are changing the future of medical care.

Drones are aircraft controlled by computers or humans on the ground.

EXPLORING THE UNREACHABLE

Roboticists design robots that visit distant or hard-to-reach locations. For example, robotics engineering makes it possible to observe the deep ocean and outer space. Robots are also designed to go into places that are inaccessible to human explorers, such as the ancient pyramids in Egypt. Roboticists even found a way to explore an active volcano! Many robotic tools are important for expanding our understanding of Earth and our solar system.

Robotics engineering helps improve our knowledge of remote oceans through inventions such as underwater robots.

AUTOMATING FACTORIES

Roboticists may look for solutions to increase efficiency, speed, and safety in factories. They design manipulators that can make a variety of products. Mechanical arms assemble many things that are part of daily life, including toys, cars, and computers. Automated processes reduce errors and lost time, which lowers costs. They also do jobs that humans once did. What are the benefits and the disadvantages of using robots in factories?

This search-and-rescue robot looks for casualties during a test run of a disaster.

Some roboticists think of ways robots might be able to find people trapped after earthquakes and other disasters.

KEEPING HUMANS SAFE

Finding ways to do tasks in settings that are accessible but not safe for humans is another focus of robotics engineering. Robots can help with the search-and-rescue missions after disasters such as earthquakes. They also go into **radioactive** areas where humans cannot survive. Drones allow militaries to scout hostile places without risking the lives of pilots. Roboticists also design robots that can clear rock barriers in mines. This avoids humans having to work with dangerous explosives. These solutions often save people's lives.

PROBLEM SOLVING

Roboticists may take part in one or more stages of the engineering design process. They often work in teams made up of experts in different subjects. The teams at the National Aeronautics and Space Administration (NASA) are a great example. NASA develops technologies related to space and to airplanes in the United States. When NASA begins a project, it starts by defining a task or problem. This is the first step of the design process.

These engineers and scientists are working on a robotic device for exploring Mars.

Define the problem: Mars is the closest planet to Earth that humans might be able to live on. The ability to send people safely to other planets does not yet exist. That has not stopped NASA and other space agencies from exploring these distant worlds. Since the 1960s, teams from around the world have designed ways to study Mars. Robotic **rovers** have made some exciting discoveries, such as the locations of ancient lakes. However, NASA was still not sure whether Mars could support life. The problem was that they needed more data about the planet's materials and processes.

Needs and limits

The next step in the design process is to research and identify criteria and constraints. Criteria are the needs of a design. For example, the device may need to perform certain tasks or meet safety standards. Constraints are the limits on the project. They include the location in which the design needs to work, materials that can be used, and the project budget.

Roboticists search for ways to help scientists study rocks and soil on Mars.

Identify criteria and constraints:
NASA worked out the details of the task. The solution needed to travel through space and land safely on Mars. It needed a way to collect a wide variety of samples. The new design also needed to analyze those materials. The rough terrain on Mars had been a problem for robots in the past. Addressing this issue was important because there was no one nearby to help if a problem arose. Constraints that limited the project included the size and weight of the robot. As size and weight increased, so did construction and launch costs. NASA had to use materials that worked well in the harsh conditions on Mars. The remote location meant that broken parts could not be repaired.

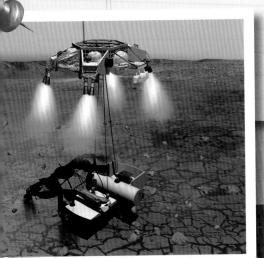

Even the best-designed robots cannot work on Mars if they do not land there safely!

INNOVATIVE IDEAS

After defining and researching the problem, brainstorming is the next step in the process. Roboticists come up with as many ideas for potential solutions as they can. There are no bad ideas during this stage!

NASA's engineering design process took place at the Jet Propulsion Lab in California.

Brainstorm ideas: Based on NASA's criteria, they knew the solution should be some form of space robot. Teams of engineers and scientists brainstormed ideas for the mechatronic system (see page 9). NASA also invited experts from outside the agency to propose ideas for scientific studies and new tools for conducting them. Some teams came up with ideas for imaging, weather, and chemical sensors. The control-systems experts came up with ideas for autonomous and remote-controlled operation. Other groups brainstormed ways to use manipulators and end effectors to collect samples. One team came up with ideas for keeping the robot from becoming stuck in sand or on rocks. They also suggested leaving a Morse code message of dots and dashes on the ground using tire tracks!

Tire tracks can leave patterns on the surface of Mars.

COMPUTER SCIENCE

Computer control systems allow roboticists to put their amazing ideas into action. Ada Lovelace designed the world's first basic computer program in Britain in 1842. She created it for Charles Babbage's mechanical calculator. In the 1940s, the U.S. Army collaborated with the University of Pennsylvania to create the first modern computer. Over the decades, computers became faster and the parts became smaller. As computers stored more data, programs could be more complex.

Ada Lovelace devoted herself to math and writing in the 1800s.

Babbage and Lovelace's work on this mechanical calculator made them computer pioneers.

HOTEL ROBOT

Robotics engineering developed alongside computer science. Today, advances in AI create new possibilities for robots. For example, IBM developed a computer with AI called Watson in 2011. Engineers and scientists at the company brainstormed ideas to display Watson's computing power. They came up with many ways to use it in robotics engineering and other fields. One of their innovative ideas led to an android providing customer service at a hotel. Watson allows the hotel robot to "think" and interact with guests. The robot can answer questions about the hotel's services and even help travelers plan their trips.

Hotel robots such as this one will improve along with future advances in AI.

A PROMISING SOLUTION

After brainstorming ideas, roboticists review all the options. They consider which ideas are most likely to meet their criteria and constraints. Then they choose the most promising solution to develop. If the first idea does not work out, roboticists select another idea to take through the process. Why do you think roboticists do not develop every option? The main reason is limited resources, such as time and money.

Select a solution: NASA chose to develop a new kind of robotic rover. Unlike previous rovers, it would conduct a variety of science experiments. They called it the Mars Science Laboratory (MSL). The robotic subsystems would use many of the ideas from the brainstorming stage. For example, NASA planned to develop a subsystem that would use laser and imaging sensors to sample rocks quickly and easily. A program would identify whether the materials were worthy of further investigation. If they were, a drill and other end effectors would collect samples for scientists to study remotely. NASA even decided to use the idea of leaving a message in Morse code on the planet's surface with the rover's tire tracks. Its distinct tracks would show the robot where it had already explored.

This artwork shows what the robotic Mars rover's rock-vaporizing laser could look like.

POWER SOURCES

When roboticists select a solution to develop, its power source is an important consideration. Batteries are the most common way to store electricity and power robotic systems. Previous Mars rovers used **solar panels** to generate power. Solar power also recharged the batteries that ran the rovers when there was no sunlight. However, conditions on Mars were challenging for solar power. The rovers could not operate during winter because of the weak sunlight. Over time, dust built up on the panels, so they were less efficient. The MSL would use **plutonium** to produce electricity. It could work year round and last for at least 687 days—one Mars year. The radioactive plutonium also created heat. It would warm the control system and keep it from freezing in the cold temperatures on Mars.

This robot is powered by solar panels that sit on top of its frame.

This team is working together to prepare the power source for the new Mars robotic rover.

MODELS AND PROTOTYPES

Roboticists develop a potential solution by creating models of the design. They start by drawing plans on paper or in computer-design programs. Roboticists may also prepare computer models for **simulated** tests. Finally, they build prototypes, which are physical models made for testing. Usually, the first materials used are inexpensive and simple. This is because roboticists expect to rebuild prototypes after testing them.

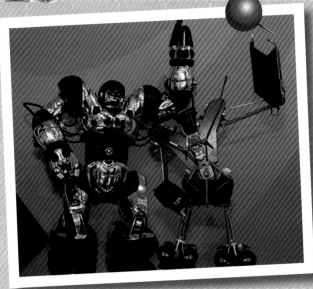

The robot on the left is the final version of the prototype shown on the right.

Developing prototypes: NASA began the prototype stage for the MSL by creating concept drawings. Next, they prepared computer models of each part and subsystem. After the entire system was fine-tuned, teams built prototypes. For some parts, they used materials that were lighter in weight than the materials they would eventually use. This helped them simulate the reduced force of **gravity** on Mars during testing. The designs of some parts were up to 10 years old. This meant they had been proven to work over time. NASA knew there would be no way to fix anything once the rover left Earth. For this reason, they built and tested many parts separately. Then they assembled the parts into prototype subsystems for more testing.

The Scarecrow was built to perform well in a setting similar to the one on Mars.

A subsystem for the MSL: The Scarecrow was a prototype subsystem that only included wheels and a frame that would support the MSL. NASA assembled the entire prototype after each subsystem was tested and refined. (There's more information about testing on pages 22-23.)

Partnerships

Roboticists collaborated with more than 1,000 people on the design of the MSL. Clear communication kept the project moving forward. NASA also teamed up with other space agencies and companies from around the world. For example, the Canadian Space Agency funded a tool designed by scientists at the University of Guelph in Ontario. The instrument worked like an X-ray machine and detected the materials in rock samples. These partnerships allowed agencies such as NASA to share expertise.

ROBONAUT 2

The Robonaut 2 project is another example of partnerships at work. General Motors and NASA designed this android for use on the International Space Station. The same robotics technologies developed to assist astronauts could also become part of the automated manufacturing processes.

American engineer and astronaut Karen Nyberg poses with Robonaut 2 in space.

TEST AND IMPROVE

Once roboticists have a prototype, they plan and conduct tests for it. Then they review the test results to see if it worked well. Roboticists expect to discover problems with their designs during testing. They do not view these issues as failures. Instead, roboticists see them as ways to improve the design at the next stage.

Robotic rovers are tested to see how well they can travel through Mars-like soil.

Testing prototypes: NASA used a wide variety of testing methods for their Mars rover. For example, an outdoor area called the Mars Yard simulated the surface of Mars. This allowed the design team to test how the Scarecrow mobility system would handle the terrain on Mars. Another test area had a vacuum chamber in which air was pumped out to reproduce the conditions in space. Test beds were indoor platforms set up with Mars-like environments. They allowed testers to see how the rover would perform in the various conditions it might encounter on Mars. This stage was thorough because if just one part broke down in space, the entire system would fail.

The stages of building, testing, and improving prototypes repeat in a cycle. Roboticists make **trade-offs** as they improve the design. This means they set aside one or more criteria to fulfill a more important need. The cycle continues until roboticists **optimize** the design. At that point, it functions as well as it can. If the design does not solve the problem identified at the start of the process, roboticists develop another solution.

Improving the design: NASA optimized each part of the MSL. Then they assembled the parts into subsystems that were tested and improved. The size and weight of the model rover were major constraints. Trade-offs made it smaller and lighter. For example, NASA removed a camera that would have viewed Mars as the rover landed. The camera required too many resources and was less important than tools needed to study the surface. The build-test-improve cycle took more than six years. The final mechatronic system was five times larger than previous Mars rovers. The MSL included 17 cameras, a backup control system, and a manipulator that could brush, drill, and scoop.

A NASA engineer tests the movements of the MSL's jointed manipulator and end effectors.

SHARE THE SOLUTION

The engineering design process ends with sharing the solution. Roboticists describe the process in **journals** and at conferences. This includes communicating the development of separate parts and subsystems. At this point, roboticists can send the design into production. They could also sell it to a company or government agency.

Communicate the process: Space agencies, roboticists, and media around the world were just some of the people following NASA's design process. The American space agency made progress reports during this high-profile project. When the robotic rover was complete, NASA shared technical papers describing the development of each subsystem.

On August 5, 2012, the MSL landed on Mars and began its mission. The rover has a one-of-a-kind design. NASA is unlikely to produce more robots just like it. However, the designs of its subsystems could become part of other robotic systems.

The MSL rover was named Curiosity. The robot took this selfie after it landed on Mars!

ASIMO

Another widely shared robotics engineering solution is the Advanced Step in Innovative Mobility (ASIMO). Roboticists at Honda in Japan began developing this android in 1986. They completed the first version in 2000. Honda keeps improving ASIMO and sharing details about the process. The robot's function is to assist humans. In the future, it may do tasks for people who cannot move their arms or legs. ASIMO could also help visually impaired people move around safely. It even performs sign language. Honda plans to sell the robot for home use someday. For now, ASIMO demonstrates its abilities at conferences.

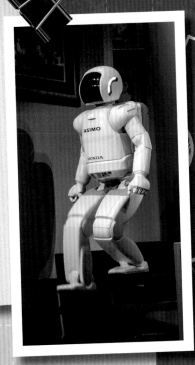

ASIMO is one of the world's most famous androids.

Robots in the news

What stories have you noticed about robotics innovations in the media? Maybe you heard about Alice Wong meeting American President Barack Obama in 2015 using a remote-controlled robot that sent and received real-time videos. This technology helped Wong, the founder of the Disability Visibility Project, to communicate with guests at the White House from her own home. You may have also seen hitchBOT in the news. Its Canadian designers created this autonomous robot to interact with human strangers and explore. hitchBOT hitchhiked more than 6,200 miles (10,000 km) across Canada in 2014.

A robot helped Alice Wong meet President Obama!

hitchBOT was designed to appear friendly. It also visited Germany and Netherlands.

DESIGN CHALLENGE

Follow the engineering design process to make your own manipulator! Its end effector subsystem might grip, attach to, or even paint objects. You can use everyday items for building materials. Look around for old rulers, telescopic or jointed rods, or broken toys. Office supplies such as cardboard, scissors, fasteners, string, and magnets may be useful, too.

1. Define: Your task is to make a mechanical arm with an end effector that can perform any function you choose. If you are working with a friend, collaborate on describing the function.

2. Investigate: Consider the criteria and constraints of your manipulator. For example, it should be strong enough to perform the task and move smoothly. The materials available may limit your design. The size of your workspace may limit the size of your manipulator.

3. Brainstorm: Think up as many design ideas as possible. Look at your own arm and hand for inspiration. Think about how other body parts or machines move, too. Get creative with end-effector ideas, such as magnets, clips, or paint brushes. Use notes and sketches to expand on your ideas. Describe as many details as possible.

4. Select a solution: Review your list of ideas. Which one do you think has the most potential to meet your criteria and constraints? Select the most promising idea to develop.

5. **Build a prototype**: Draw plans for your design. Finalize each detail, then construct a prototype. There will probably be flaws in the first version of your mechanical arm and end effector. You can fix them later.

6. **Testing**: Put your manipulator to the test! Take notes about how it performs the task you want it to do. Confirm your results by repeating the tests.

Designing innovative manipulators is an important part of robotics engineering.

7. **Improvements**: Review your test results. What parts of the system worked well? What changes to the inputs would improve your output? Do you need to make any trade-offs to meet the criteria from step two? Refine the design and retest it. Keep optimizing your prototype until it works as well as it can. Remember, roboticists may scrap the first idea and choose another possible solution to build, test, and refine.

8. **Communicate the solution**: Record the story of your engineering design process. Create instructions that would allow someone else to make your design. Explain your process to a friend or relative in a taped or live presentation.

FUTURE OF THE FIELD

Roboticists already design solutions for the medical field. For example, they make robots that doctors control to perform surgeries. Engineers and scientists are developing many other ideas for future use. Tiny robots with snake-like bodies could investigate problems inside human body systems. Some devices may travel in the bloodstream. They could destroy dangerous blood clots or clean buildups of materials that cause heart attacks. Other robots may find and repair cells that cause diseases. Another idea is a robotic suit that will allow paralyzed people to walk.

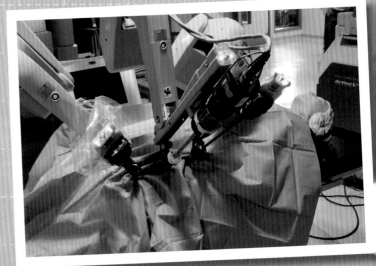

Robotics engineering has helped to make complex, remote-controlled surgery possible.

Robots the size of a tiny blood cell could be used to treat diseases in the future.

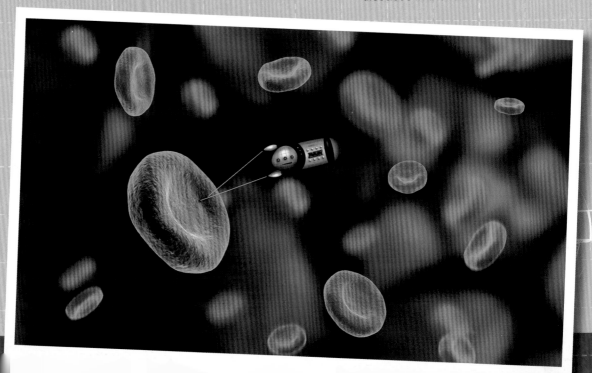

SELF-DRIVING CARS

Google claims its self-driving car is already better than humans at driving safely.

In 2004, an agency in the U.S. Department of Defense held the first long-distance, autonomous robotic vehicle race. They wanted to inspire innovation and creativity in robotics engineering. No one won the first prize of $1 million because none of the cars were able to complete the race. Roboticists improved their designs and five vehicles drove the whole route the next year. Work on self-driving vehicles continues in labs and on roads around the world. It may not be long before you see an autonomous car driving past you!

Ethical concerns

Robotics engineering has raised many **ethical** concerns. For example, drones may invade people's privacy. Some people believe that robots could replace too many human workers. As roboticists make advances with AI control systems, many kinds of jobs could be automated. How far do you think we should go in replacing humans with robots? Androids that appear to have human emotions pose another potential problem. Their programming could take advantage of vulnerable people instead of helping them. Some roboticists create robotic weapons. Under what conditions do you think it is right to arm a drone or an autonomous robotic soldier? In the future, do you think we need to worry about what robots will do—or about the actions of the people who design them?

Would you trust a military robot's sense-think-act process to keep humans safe? Why or why not?

LEARNING MORE

BOOKS

Bow, James. *Maker Projects for Kids Who Love Robotics*. Crabtree Publishing, 2016.

Ceceri, Kathy. *Robotics: Discover the Science and Technology of the Future*. Nomad Press, 2012.

Domaine, Helena. *Robotics*. Lerner Publications, 2006.

Mercer, Bobby. *The Robot Book*. Chicago Review Press, 2014.

Swanson, Jennifer. *Everything Robotics*. National Geographic Children's Books, 2016.

ONLINE

http://kidsahead.com/subjects/1-robotics/cool_jobs
Learn about careers in different areas of robotics engineering.

www.nasa.gov/audience/foreducators/robotics/careercorner
Read profiles for careers related to robotics engineering for space at NASA's Career Corner page.

www.instructables.com/id/Your-First-Robot
Check out step-by-step instructions for making simple robots on the project-sharing website Instructables.

http://mars.nasa.gov/msl
Find news, photos, videos, and more about the MSL rover's mission on Mars.

PLACES TO VISIT

Canada Aviation and Space Museum, Ottawa, Ontario
See the original Canadarm, one of Canada's most famous examples of robotic engineering.
http://casmuseum.techno-science.ca

MIT Museum, Cambridge, Massachusetts
Visit the ongoing *Robots and Beyond: Exploring Artificial Intelligence at MIT* exhibit.
http://web.mit.edu/museum/exhibitions/robots.html

The Tech Museum of Innovation, San Jose, California
Get hands-on with sensors, control systems, and actuators in the Social Robots gallery.
www.thetech.org

GLOSSARY

actuator A mechanical device that moves one or more parts

android A robot with a human-like form

artificial intelligence (AI) A machine's ability to mimic human intelligence and emotions

autonomous Describes a machine that controls its own actions through programming

collaborate To work together

control system A set of computer parts that work together to process data

drone A remote-controlled or autonomous aircraft

effector A part of a robot that takes action and can affect its surroundings

ethical Relating to the rules of what is right and wrong

gravity A force that acts between objects (or masses) to pull them together

innovative Describes something that is inventive or ground breaking

journal A magazine in which professionals who are focused on a particular field share information and the results of their work

optimize Improve the function of a design through trade-offs that balance criteria and constraints

paralyzed Unable to move

pioneer The first person who develops an idea or technique

plutonium A radioactive chemical produced during the manufacture of nuclear products

program To provide a computer with instructions for tasks to perform; a series of commands that instruct a computer to perform a task

pulley A simple machine that includes a wheel connected to a chain or rope, which moves attached objects

radioactive Emits a dangerous type of energy wave that can harm living things

rover A robotic vehicle often used in space exploration

sensor A device that detects information from its surroundings

simulate To make a representation of how something will work, often using a computer

solar panel A plate-like part of a system that converts the Sun's energy into electricity

space shuttle A vehicle that brings astronauts and cargo from Earth to space and back again

subsystem A group of interconnected and interactive parts that perform a task as part of a larger system

technology A machine or tool created by engineers or scientists to solve problems

telescopic Describes an object that can be made longer or shorter through sliding parts

trade-off Setting aside of one criterion so that a more important criterion is met

INDEX